**Trading St
Fractal Co
on the Futu
and Forex**

Four Basic ST Patterns
800% or More in Two Month

Vladimir Poltoratskiy

Copyright 2017 Vladimir Poltoratskiy

License Notes

This e-book is licensed for your personal enjoyment only. This e-book may not be re-sold or given away to other people. If you would like to share this book with another person, please purchase an additional copy for each recipient. If you're reading this book and did not purchase it, or it was not purchased for your use only, then please return to your favorite e-book retailer and purchase your own copy. Thank you for respecting the hard work of this author.

Risk Warning

Carrying out trading operations on the financial markets with marginal financial instruments has a high level of risk and may lead to the loss of invested funds. Before you start trading, please take all conceivable precautions and ensure that you fully recognize all risks and have all relevant knowledge for each trade. None of the trading recommendations provided in this book should be considered a provision of individual consultation for concrete investment decisions. The given recommendations can be used only as an illustration of the described principles. The author is not liable for any profits or losses that may be caused directly or indirectly by using the information presented in this book. The author describes the rules of trade that he has learned from his personal, long-term experience on the currency market. These may not necessarily reflect the views of other experts in this field who have used other trading strategies.

Table of Contents

From the Author 4
Fundamentals of ST Patterns Strategy 5
Four Basic ST Patterns 9
Additional Parameters of ST Patterns 20
Analysis of the EUR/USD Currency Pair 39
Mind and Subconscious 57
Answer to the Question 60
Conclusion 63
Contact 64

From the Author

This book concludes the publication of material on a new, effective ST Patterns Strategy based on Fractal Corridors. An open method of technical analysis is applicable for short- and medium-term work in many liquid markets, including, for example, Forex, Futures, CFD or Crypto currency.

To simplify the construction of models, the rules for working with four basic ST Patterns that are common for all graphic combinations, have been singled out. The exclusion from the game of completed Corridors facilitates the analysis of complex models.

A detailed technical analysis of the EUR/USD chart for two months demonstrates a result equal to + 800% of the initial deposit. The received profit can be much higher if you consider the influence of economic indicators, which are published under the schedule.

The final part of the book is devoted to psychological difficulties that can hamper one's success in the exchange game.

For more information about the ST Patterns Strategy you can visit my website https://stpatterns.com: indicators, videos, daily trading strategy, answers to questions...

Fundamentals of ST Patterns Strategy

For those who are not familiar with the content of the first two books *Trading Code is Open* and *Forex Strategy*, I will briefly repeat the fundamentals of ST Patterns Strategy before moving on to the new material. Structural Patterns reflect the structure of almost all market movements divided into parts and are completed at the moment of reaching the Target price. Technical models, following each other, signal traders to take action in the present. At the heart of their emergence is the reaction of market participants to the critical situations that are constantly emerging in the market.

The first thing you need to do to build a trading system is to determine the conditions for an opening position. In various trading systems, there are methods of buying or selling when a trend line breaks after the formation of various graphic models or a certain combination of graphic candles. The lines of various indicators—for example, Bollinger bands or simple average or exponentially smoothed moving averages—can be taken into account.

Traders can enter the transaction near significant round price levels and even on a whim. The ST Patterns Strategy uses a simple and logical method for opening a position after breaking through the price peaks or recessions. To easily identify and determine these levels visually, three candlestick fractal indicators are used.

A logical explanation of why players' emotions push prices in the direction of a breakthrough is described in detail in the first book, *Trading Code is Open*. Figure 1 shows the outline of the emergence of a Support Level, which in the ST Patterns Strategy is called the Fracture Level.

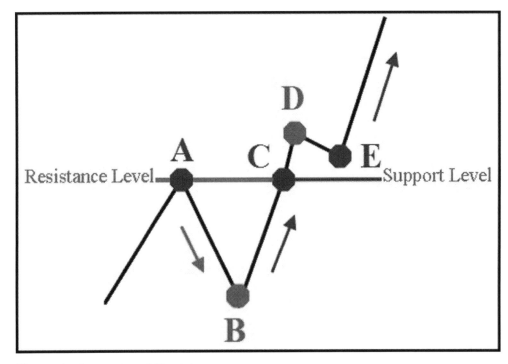

Figure 1: Support and Resistance

Often the continuation of the movement toward a breakthrough depends on the participation in the game of speculative capital. Professional traders use these situations to generate profits and push prices toward a breakthrough. The further the price goes from the breakout place, the higher the revenue from the transaction will be. Figure 2 shows a classic picture drawn by stock speculators.

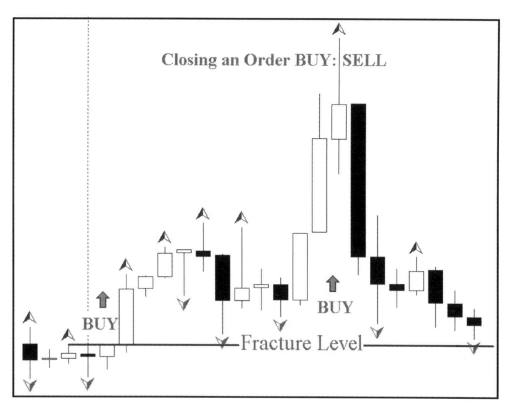

Figure 2: The Fractal Level Breakthrough

Fractal peaks and slumps in the graph are shown using the Fractals ST Patterns indicator. This indicator is available for free download at http://stpatterns.com/indicators-parameters/ or https://www.mql5.com/en/market.

On the hourly chart, you can see how the price first came back to the pierced level after a breakdown of the fractal level, and then the second wave raised the market to a new height. The big players, who earned good money on this day, created this second strong movement. After these players fixed their profits and closing positions, the price returned to the level of launch, visually demonstrating the speculative nature of the movement upward.

This example shows the main essence of short-term and medium-term exchange trade. This pattern is repeated and will be repeated on the charts of many liquid trading instruments in the Forex, CFD, and Futures markets. However, for some reason, this simple example is difficult to find in numerous textbooks on stock trading.

However, even understanding the basic principle of working in the market, a trader needs to be able to solve a problem with several unknown values. To build a trading system, you need to know the value for fixing the breakthrough of the fractal level in order to determine the rules for installing the Stop Loss Order and the Take Profit Order. It is also necessary to understand how to act during times of premature reversal and uncertainty in the market. Figure 3 again shows this graph with the designation of unknown values.

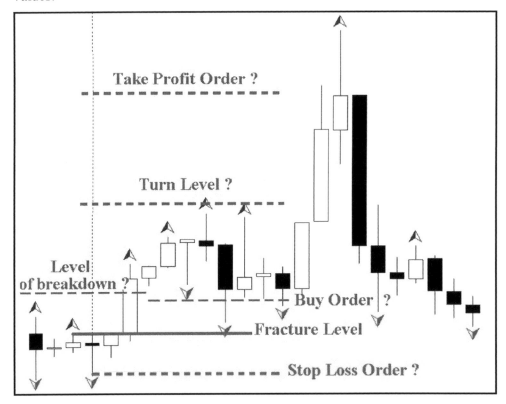

Figure 3: Variable Parameters of the Trading System

Solving a problem with a large number of unknown values is not easy. However, all traders need to do this to build any trading system. In this case, the values of the parameters may differ for each trading instrument.

To determine the values of unknowns, you need to analyze the repetitive graphic models of the selected tool and, to start, approximately determine the possible values. The exact parameters of the system are determined after testing and analyzing historical data from the past few years.

Why are these levels shown in the graph important for the technical analysis of charts? Consider the example of the four major ST Patterns. The rules of work for the appearance of each model are logically justified and confirmed by numerous tests of historical data and their long-term use in practice.

Four Basic ST Patterns

All ST Patterns are formed according to the rules adopted for the four main graphic models: **ST Direct Movement Pattern**, **ST False Movement Pattern**, **ST Reverse Movement Pattern**, and **ST Counter Movement Pattern**. The remaining ST Patterns often only consist of combinations of these four models. Figures 2 and 3 show the first basic **ST Direct Movement Pattern**.

ST Direct Movement Pattern

This pattern is one of the most common on the charts of liquid trading instruments. A schematic image of this pattern is shown in Figure 4. All the patterns shown here have their symmetrical counterpart rotated 180 degrees from the horizontal axis.

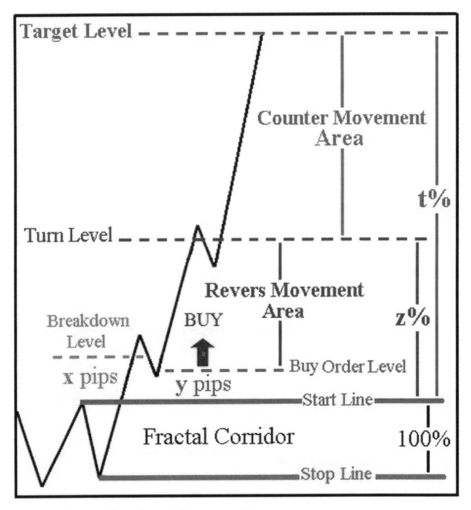

Figure 4: Scheme ST Direct Movement Pattern

The ST Direct Movement Pattern is formed when the price after purchase reaches the Target Level without Counter Movements. The model can be seen at different time periods. In the Futures and Forex markets, the best results are obtained by applying this pattern on the hourly chart, where the fast **ST Direct Movement Pattern** can reach the Take Profit Level within a few hours. The slow version of this model sometimes takes a few days to move to the Target. Hourly charts allow the trader to calmly assess market movements and make informed decisions.

According to the rules of building, the ST Patterns Fracture Level is designated as the Start Line. The Stop Line passes through the level of the opposite fractal that is closest to the punctured one. The Stop Loss Order is placed at or near the Stop Line Level. For more details about installing the

Stop Loss Order depending on the direction of the previous pattern's movement, see the book *Forex Strategy: ST Patterns Trading Manual*.

Between the Start Line and the Stop Line Level is Fractal Corridor. The height of the Fractal Corridor is equal to the distance between the Start and Stop Lines and is measured in the quotation points of the trading instrument. The height of the Fractal Corridor is assumed to be 100%.

After the price of the Breakdown Level is reached, the Fractal Level breaks through, and then the deal opens on the Buy Order Level. The Breakdown Level is indicated in the diagram with a green dotted line. The distance x from the Start Line to the Breakdown Level, measured in points, is important in order to exclude a lot of losing trades from the game. More details of these situations will be shown in the example of the second main **ST False Movement Pattern.**

The value of the variable x is individual for each trading instrument and, as a rule, directly proportional to the volatility and the time period of the chart. For many currency pairs in the Forex market, opening a position is more profitable outside the Fractal Corridor, using a small price rollback after the breakthrough of the Start Line. If the trading instrument often makes deep corrections, then transactions can also be opened inside the Fractal Corridor.

To determine the amount of x sufficient for fixing the breakdown, it is necessary to test the historical data of the selected trading instrument using different values of the variable. To begin with, you need to analyze the behavior of prices at the moments of breakthroughs of fractal levels before obvious subsequent movements in the direction of the breakout. At present, for many liquid currency pairs, active trading is conducted using hourly and 5-minute charts. This became clear after numerous tests of various time parameters.

Theoretically, it is possible to use the ST Patterns Strategy on any time schedule. However, the 5-minute and hour intervals are very appropriate for short- and medium-term work and, therefore, probably attracts large speculative capital.

Next, you need to consider the moment of a breakthrough on a smaller scale, for example, on minute charts. Often, the actual penetration of the Fractal Level increases volatility, and there are high candles on minute or five-minute charts. Various options for opening a position can be checked for a longer historical period. By changing the value of the variable x and repeating the tests, you can find its optimal value. A reliable result for the hourly chart can be obtained by investigating the behavior of prices over the past few years.

For example, for hourly three candlestick fractal patterns for the present EUR/USD pair, I use the value of x equal to 7.6 pips, while for the GBP/USD pair, x is equal to 13 pips. It is curious that according to the rules of numerology, the experimentally found optimal value of 7.6 also gives a total of 13. The value of this number is often associated with the completion of the old cycle and the beginning of the new one. The 13th lasso in the tarot maps means death, and through this connection, it probably has many unpleasant associations.

However, there is nothing wrong in the destruction of the fractal level, and often this event opens the way for a new movement. Perhaps the value of this number will speed up the search for the value of x for other trading instruments. As shown in the first book, *Trading Code is Open*, and then in the trading manual, *Forex Trading*, the use of a slightly different value for this variable can also be effective. This value persists for many years. Therefore, you should not often change the parameters of the system without making sure that the market has really changed.

The variable y specifies the level for opening a trade. This value also depends on the nature of the trading instrument and the tactics of working with the ST Patterns Strategy. For the H1, EUR/USD pair, a good result is the opening of the position on a small price rollback after the breakthrough of the Fractal Level.

The next variable, z, determines the distance from the Start Line Level to the Turn Level. This value is measured as a percentage of the height of the Fractal Corridor. A Counter Movement occurring before the price reaches the Turn Level often does not receive continuation, and it is better to miss it. If the Turn Level is reached, the probability of reversal increases, and this circumstance should be taken into account when creating rules for working with ST Patterns.

Logically, the importance of the value z can be explained by the example of the EUR/USD currency pair. For this pair, the optimal value for this variable is approximately 210%. At this level, the profit is more than twice the loss, given the opening of the transaction just above the Start Line Level. The smaller value of the ratio of profit to loss makes the risk of loss too high. According to broker statistics, successful traders receive revenue in less than half of all their transactions. The profit can also be reduced due to spread, price slippage, or a small height of Fractal Corridors.

Players who close positions before the price reaches the level of 210% of the height of the Fractal Corridor are likely to lose their deposits. Therefore, the influence of this group of players on the movement of quotes does not often lead to changes in the direction of prices. Long tests of historical data confirm this statement. Therefore, the ST Patterns Strategy does not foresee closing the deal on the EUR/USD pair until the price reaches a level that is less than 210% of the height of the Fractal Corridor.

Closing position above the 210% level allows a trader to keep his deposit, and this group of players sometimes manages to deploy the trading instrument in the opposite direction due to their actions. For example, testing the pair EUR/USD, H1 with a target of 230% showed a good result for several years with the exception of 2013. Therefore, price levels, starting at 210% or more, are taken into account as a place for a possible market reversal.

The variable t measures the distance from the Start Line Level to the Target Level as a percentage of the height of the Fractal Corridor. Traders use a different distance to the Target. This magnitude can be affected by the manifestations of players' individual psychological qualities, such as patience or the fear of losing their profits. The value of the Take Profit can also differ between an intra day and medium-term trading system.

To obtain long-lasting good trading results, the distance from the opening position to the Target should be several times greater than before the Stop Loss Order. In other words, the profit should be several times greater than the possible loss. The ST Patterns Strategy involves the installation of the Take Profit Order at a level that is several times the height of the Fractal Corridor. For the EUR/USD currency pair, the optimal value of the variable t is equal to 380-400%. At the same time, positive trading results can give other values, in which the profit is more than twice as much as the loss.

The value of the Target Level as well as the Turn Level may differ for different trading instruments. If the quotes of a trading instrument after a breakout are often returned to the inside of Fractal Corridors and deals are opened on this deep rollback, smaller percentage levels are used in the gaming strategy. For markets moving rapidly in one direction, the Target Level can be more than 400%. You can find the optimal value of this variable through experimentation.

ST False Movement Pattern

Next, consider the importance of the value of the variable x in the example of the second basic **ST False Movement Pattern**, whose schema is shown in Figure 5.

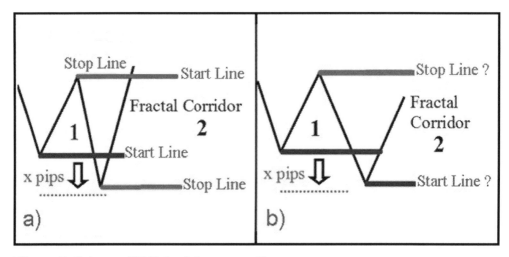

Figure 5: Scheme ST False Movement Pattern

The **ST False Movement Pattern** is the main pattern from which all Starting Patterns are composed. Knowledge of these graphic models is necessary to exclude a lot of losing trades from the game. In fact, if you open a position immediately, as soon as the price crosses the Fractal Level, you can lose significant funds on the false breakdowns.

With the formation of this pattern, the initial downward movement turned out to be false. Often, when it overcomes the Start Line, the price cannot move further by an amount sufficient to fracture the Fractal Level, and it unfolds in the opposite direction. The ST False Movement pattern is formed completely at the moment that the Start Line price crosses Corridor № 1 or a new lower fractal becomes fully formed.

a) The **ST False Movement Pattern** is completed at the moment that the price crosses the Stop Line Level at Corridor № 1. At the same time, Corridor №1 loses its meaning, and Corridor № 2 enters the game.

b) The **ST False Movement Pattern** is completed when the new lower fractal becomes fully formed. After the formation of the pattern, Corridor № 1 loses its value, and the new Breakdown Level is measured from the Start Line of Corridor № 2. Where exactly the Start Line will be located will become clear after the price crosses the border of Corridor № 2.

The difference between Figure 5a) and 5b) is better seen in the example of the real graphs presented in Figure 6.

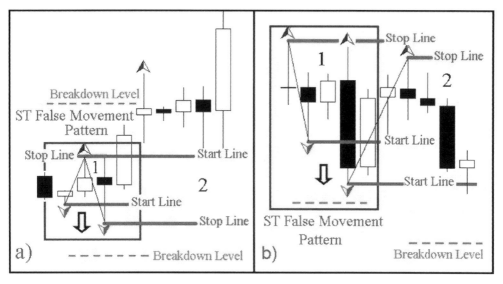

Figure 6: ST False Movement Pattern

a) The price crosses the fractal level of Corridor № 1 down. However, it does not reach Breakdown Level, and when it turns around, it breaks the opposite Fractal Level, completing this pattern. In this situation, the premature opening of the Sell Order would have caused the trader a loss. Rarely is there a situation when such a move down and up occurs during the formation of only one candle.

b) Having overcome the Start Line Level at Corridor № 1, the price rolled back and created a new lower fractal, completing the **ST False Movement pattern** with Corridor № 1 at the bottom. After the breakdown of the Start Line price of Corridor № 2, the new Breakdown Level will help filter out the possible false movement.

The **ST False Movement Pattern** can be repeated several times in a row or create graphic combinations with other ST Patterns. The model can appear anywhere in the chart when the price crosses the Start Line but can not overcome it by the amount of x pips.

ST Reverse Movement Pattern

After reaching the price Breakdown Level, set at a level predetermined to enter the market, the position is opened. The next basic ST Pattern is formed before reaching the Turn Level, when the market changes its direction and the price crosses the Stop Line Level. In this case, it is more profitable to take a loss than to prematurely get out of a deal in which the profit can exceed the loss several times. The **ST Reverse Movement Pattern** is shown in Figure 7.

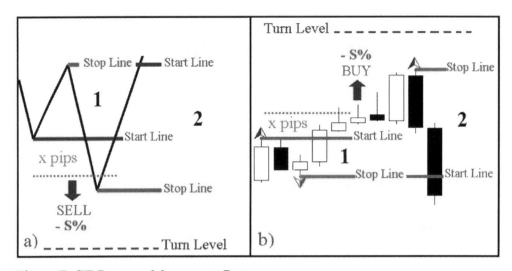

Figure 7: ST Reverse Movement Pattern

a) The **ST Reverse Movement Pattern** reflects the pattern for the initial lower breakdown of the Fractal Level of Corridor № 1. The market takes place in the Reverse Movement Area without reaching the Turn Level. The model ends when the Stop Loss Order is triggered. At this point, Corridor № 1 loses its value, and the new countdown starts from Corridor № 2 levels.

b) The price has overcome the Fractal Level upward enough to create the Fracture Level. After that, the Buy Order was opened. However, before reaching the point of the Turn Level, the market turned down and overcame the Stop Line of Corridor № 1. The trader in this situation is forced to accept a loss equal to S%. The ST Patterns Strategy calculates a possible loss as a percentage of the deposit.

Some trading instruments, for example, the GBP/USD currency pair, have the peculiarity of pursuing Stop Loss Orders located near the Stop Line, and then they continue moving in the original direction.

When working with such tools, it is better to place the Stop Loss Order outside the corridor. In this case, a slight crossing of the Stop Line price may not lead to the cancellation of the Corridor and the Stop Loss Order. Accordingly, the **ST Reverse Movement Pattern** is not formed. In this case, Corridor № 1 loses its value only after the price reaches its Stop Loss Order Level. This condition must also be taken into account when determining the completion time of other patterns when crossing the Stop Line Level.

The **ST Reverse Movement Pattern** as well as the **ST False Movement Pattern** can be repeated or can create combinations with other major ST Patterns. Knowing the rules of working with this graphic model, a trader is always able to recognize it in the composition of more complex combinations. They will be shown a little later. Now, we consider the fourth and final major ST Pattern.

ST Counter Direct Movement Pattern

Scheme ST Counter Direct Movement Pattern is shown in Figure 8.

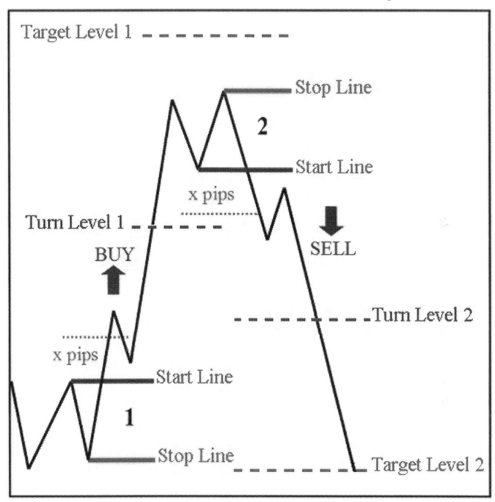

Figure 8: Scheme ST Counter Direct Movement Pattern

Movement with Fractal Corridor № 1 in the base exceeded Turn Level 1. Then, before reaching Target Level 1, the price broke down Fractal Corridor № 2. Unlike the previous major patterns, there are two active Fractal Corridors, each with their own significant Turn and Target Levels. As with previous models, if the reverse movement reaches the Start Line Level of Corridor № 1 or Stop Loss Order Level 1 in volatile markets, Corridor № 1 and all its levels lose their significance.

This pattern is completed when the price reaches Target Level 2, which may be higher than Corridor № 1. After completion, both Corridors lose their relevance, and a new countdown of the next ST Pattern begins. Figure 9 shows the **ST Counter Direct Movement Pattern** on the hourly chart.

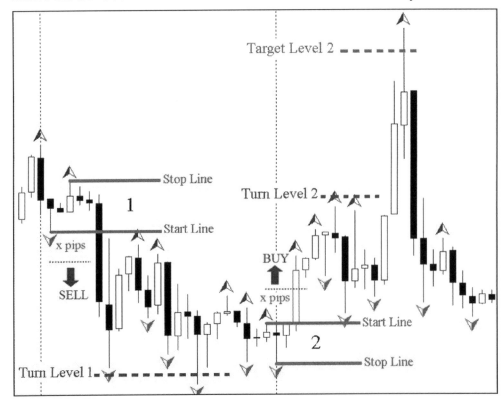

Figure 9: ST Counter Direct Movement Pattern

The **ST Counter Direct Movement Pattern** was formed within two days. The tactical actions for responding to the appearance of this model can be different. The best option for working with the EUR/USD pair was to close the initial position while simultaneously opening a new one in the opposite direction at the Buy Order Level.

There is a trading device for opening a counter position without closing the initial one. This option will be more advantageous if the counter movement does not develop and the price reaches the Target at Corridor № 1. Given the nature of the trading instrument's behavior, one can choose the most profitable tactic for working with this model.

So, we examined how the four basic ST Patterns are formed. The remaining graphic combinations are either a combination of these models or are built according to the rules described above. Understanding the logical principles of working with the basic ST Patterns, it is not necessary to remember the names of other models. It is sufficient to follow the price schedule consistently, eliminating the completed Corridors and implementing the adopted tactical actions for each combination.

Additional Parameters of ST Patterns

To simplify working with the ST Patterns Strategy, further refinements and explanations will be given in the description for those patterns that have caused questions or difficulties for traders who have dealt with them. Examples of the formation of complex ST Patterns describe their features and simpler ways of determining them by using the rules of the basic ST Patterns.

Starting ST Patterns

Fairly simple Starting ST Patterns did not seem to cause questions from readers when they were identified on the charts; thus, it is difficult to add anything new to their early description. Figure 10 shows ST Double and Triple False Movement Patterns.

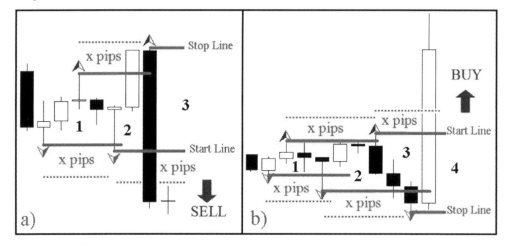

Figure 10: ST Double and Triple False Movement Patterns

a) In this situation, the ST Double False Movement Pattern is quickly completed when the Start Line price intersects Corridor № 3. Further price movement leads to the discovery of the Sell Order. Attempts to predict the direction of prices make the player dependent on these fantasies and may prevent them from reacting quickly to market reversals like this.

b) When this pattern is formed, the price makes a false break of fractal levels three times in a row. The ST Triple False Movement Pattern ended after the price intersected with the Start Line of Fractal Corridor № 4. In the future, rapid growth of quotes leads to the opening of the Buy Order. Often, such a model appears before the release of important fundamental data.

In both cases, the trader only works with one last **ST False Movement Pattern**, excluding ceased-to-act-Corridors from the game. False movements can appear in low liquid markets and more than three times in a row. However, if you understand the principle of their formation, it should not be difficult to identify such combinations on the charts.

Sometimes the price from the first time cannot overcome the fractal levels in one direction. In this case, several Fractal Corridors are formed. Basically, there are two to four steps in the formation of this model. However, it is occasionally possible to have more steps in a low liquid market. Figure 11 shows the ST Stairs Pattern on the hourly charts.

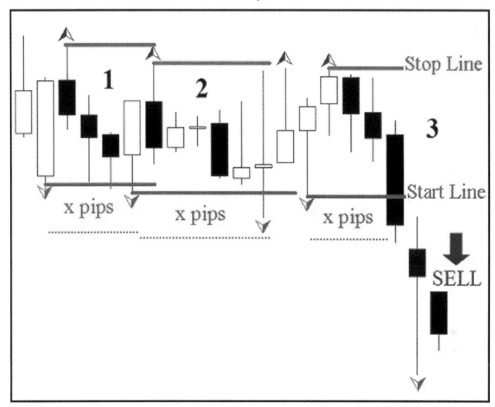

Figure 11: ST Stairs Pattern

Only in the third attempt does the price manage to overcome Fractal Level Corridor № 3 by the amount of x pips and complete this pattern formation. When working with this model, the distance x pips is better measured from each new Fractal Level, rather than, for example, from the Start Line level of Corridor № 1. Correspondingly, the Stop Line of Corridor № 3 coincides with the opposite, closest to the penetration point Fractal Level. After the formation of each new lower fractal, a new Fractal Corridor appears, and the previous one ceases to function.

It is logical to assume that the Fracture Level is more significant with respect to the Fractal Levels that were not overcome by the price of x pips. Numerous tests of various variants of work with this model have confirmed this assumption, making it a rule for working with this ST Pattern. Thus, only one last **ST False Movement Pattern** is used for analysis. Moreover, only after the model is fully formed can we count the number of steps as well as give the model a name.

All Starting ST Patterns consist of one basic **ST False Movement Pattern**, which is the most common graphic model on the market. Like the pattern itself, its combinations can appear anywhere in the chart.

Unlike the combinations of the main **ST Reverse Movement Pattern** shown below, starting models do not bring a loss to the trader.

Initial ST Patterns

ST Double, Triple, or more Reverse Movement Patterns consist of a repeating basic **ST Reverse Movement Pattern**. The ST Double Reverse Movement Pattern is shown in Figure 12.

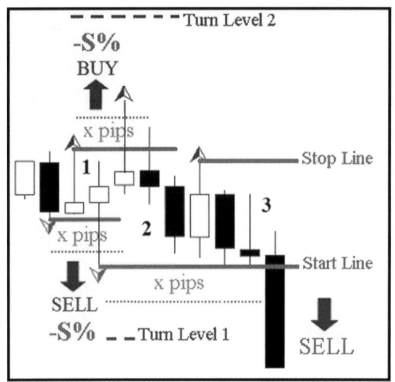

Figure 12: ST Double Reverse Movement Pattern

In the formation of this model, the price changes its direction twice after passing the distance x pips from Fractal Levels, and twice in a row it brings a loss. The ST Double Reverse Movement Pattern is completed when the second Stop Loss Order and the formation of Fractal Corridor № 3 are triggered.

Such a schedule may appear before the release of an important economic indicator. The last black candle probably ends the uncertainty in the market by decisively breaking down through the Fractal Level. During periods of uncertainty in the market that arise from the emergence of important economic or political events, the appearance of the ST Triple Reverse Movement Pattern and even models with a large number of reverse movements are possible.

The *Forex Strategy* book shows the effect of periods of uncertainty on the results of trading through the example of the GBP/USD currency pair. Given the important role of fundamental events for a short-term trader, you need to closely monitor the news, and it is often better to be out of the market during such periods.

It is not uncommon to see the **ST Reverse Movement Pattern** as a more complex version of the ST Complex Reverse Movement Pattern on the graphs. This model, which caused the most questions, is shown in Figure 13.

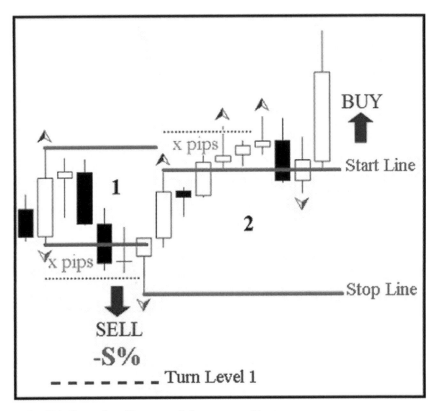

Figure 13: ST Complex Reverse Movement Pattern

Sometimes, before the price reaches the level of the initial Stop Loss Order, one or more new Fractal Corridors appear. If such patterns arise, it is better to open a new position using the Start Line of the last Corridor № 2 of the Stop Loss Order that appeared before the first transaction. The new deal opens after the price reaches Stop Loss Orders, and then it returns to the Buy Order Level of the last Corridor № 2.

Until the execution of the Stop Loss Order, the transaction does not open up. It is often premature to open a position until the price comes out of Corridor № 1. Inside Corridor, the struggle between bulls and bears unfolds with poorly predictable consequences.

At the time of the Stop Loss Order, Corridor № 1 becomes invalid, and all rights go to Corridor № 2. Sometimes the last corridor is far away, and after the Stop Loss Order at the original position, the price does not return to the Buy Order Level of this last Corridor. In this case, the opening of a new transaction will not take place. Nevertheless, the further counting of the new ST Patterns will be related to the levels of Corridor № 2.

The situation that caused the questions is taken from the *Forex Strategy* book and is shown in Figure 14.

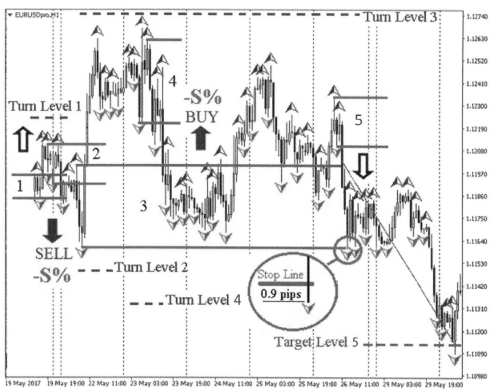

Figure 14: ST Triple Complex Reverse Movement Pattern

Corridor № 1 is less than 12 pips, and the position according to the working conditions was not opened. However, this was the first movement that did not continue and reached the Stop Loss Level of Corridor № 1. After that, Corridor №1 lost its importance. The position down is opened when the price returns to the Start Line of Corridor № 2 after the Stop Loss Order. Opening down brings a loss, and Corridor № 2 also loses its relevance. Corridor № 4 is formed until the price reaches the level of 210% of the height of Corridor № 3. Therefore, the position down can not be opened.

The price returns to the level of the Start Line of Corridor № 3 the next day. According to the rules adopted to work with this model, open the position to the top at Buy Order Level 3. Going upward and not reaching Turn Level 3, the price crosses the Stop Line Level from Corridor № 3 to 0.9 pip. At this point, all levels of Corridor № 3 lose their values. The last Corridor before the activation of the protective stop was Corridor № 5. However, the price could not rise to the level of opening, and the deal did not take place down.

25

So, every day work was done with only one model of the **ST Reverse Movement Pattern**. The total number of patterns involved in this combination can be calculated after the **ST Direct Movement Pattern** has reached Target Level 5.

The liquidity of the trading instrument and the presence of large speculative capital in the game is of great importance for the emergence and development of profitable ST Patterns. During periods of important fundamental news and events, the liquidity of the instrument falls, and the chart often shows combinations of Initial Patterns that would bring a loss.

Completion ST Patterns

Completion ST Patterns may be the most difficult to identify on the graphs. Below, the specifics of working with them will be clarified. The Scheme ST Twice Interrupted Direct Movement Pattern is shown in Figure 15.

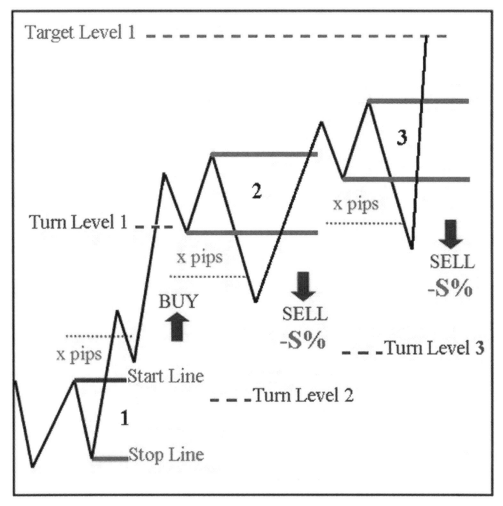

Figure 15: Scheme ST Twice Interrupted Direct Movement Pattern

For a better understanding, let's look at this pattern using the technique of opening two counter positions after turning the price higher than Turn Level 1. Under this condition, we can mark one **ST Direct Movement Pattern** with Corridor № 1 at the bottom, which has reached Target Level 1, and two **ST Reverse Movement Patterns** with Corridors № 2 and № 3 at the bottom.

After opening the position down, Corridor № 2 becomes the second worker. There are new levels, which are calculated from the height of Corridor № 2. At the same time, the levels of Corridor № 1 for the initial purchase remain relevant. Unlike Starting and Initial Patterns, when working with some Completion ST Patterns, the levels of two Corridors can be relevant at the same time.

Both **ST Reverse Movement Patterns** are completed by all the rules of this model, eliminating the importance of their Corridors after the operation of their Stop Orders. The ST Twice Interrupted Direct Movement pattern ends when the open Buy Order reaches its Target Level 1.

Until they reach Turn Level 1, counter Corridors can form one or more Starting or Initial Patterns. Models with a large number of oncoming movements are not common. The ST Thrice Interrupted Direct Movement pattern is shown in Figure 16. This pattern includes one **ST False Movement Pattern** and three counter **ST Reverse Movement Patterns**.

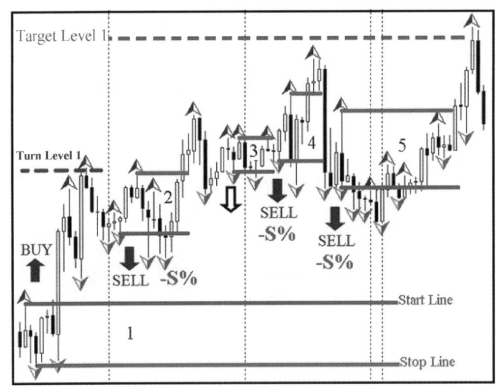

Figure 16: ST Thrice Interrupted Direct Movement Pattern

The model built on the hourly charts was formed for four days before the price reached the Target Level at Corridor № 1. After reaching Turn Level 1, breakthroughs occurred at Corridor №s 2, 4, and 5. The three **ST Reverse Movement Patterns** did not continue and caused a loss. The chart also shows a **ST False Movement Pattern** with Corridor № 3 at the bottom. The model ends when the price reaches the Target Level of Corridor № 1.

The ST Four Times Interrupted Direct Movement pattern is a rarity on the charts of liquid trading instruments. Often, after two unsuccessful attempts, the prices manage to continue the movement in the opposite direction the third time. The Scheme ST Twice Interrupted Movement with Counter Direct Movement Pattern is shown in Figure 17.

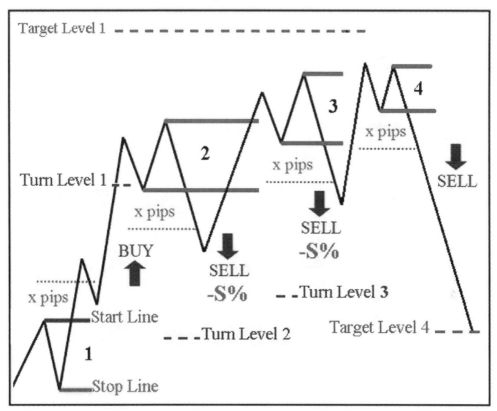

Figure 17: Scheme ST Twice Interrupted Movement with Counter Direct Movement Pattern

All Completion ST Patterns are completed at the moment the price reaches the Target and the players close their deals, fixing profits. In this situation, the combination completed the main **ST Direct Movement Pattern** with Corridor № 4 at the bottom. Given the initial direction upward, the last downward movement can be called Counter Direct. The real graph of the ST Twice Interrupted Movement with the Counter Direct Movement Pattern is shown in Figure 18.

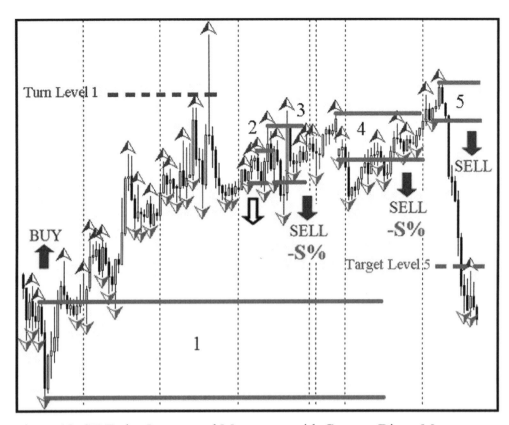

Figure 18: ST Twice Interrupted Movement with Counter Direct Movement Pattern

After the appearance of the **ST False Movement Pattern** and two **ST Reverse Movement Patterns,** players, who were disappointed in the prospects for growth, played down. The Target Level 5 that completes this model can also be located lower than the Stop Line Level of Corridor № 1.

A slightly more complicated situation occurs when three Corridors are formed simultaneously. The following two similar but different patterns are shown in Figures 19-22. The difference between these two models is in the location of the № 3 Corridors and the Target Levels at which the pattern is completed.

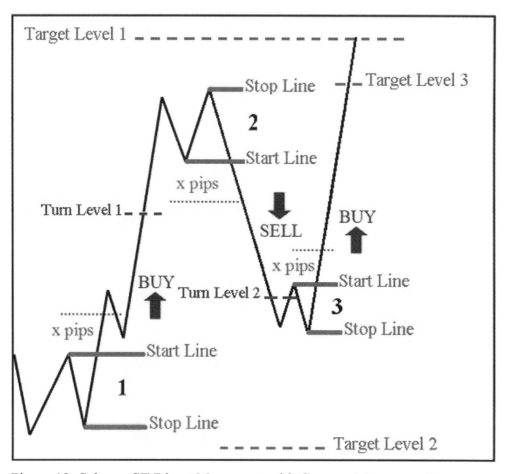

Figure 19: Scheme ST Direct Movement with Counter Movement Pattern

Having formed Corridor № 2 above Turn Level 1, the price turned down and overcame Start Line Level 2 by x pips. This situation is similar to the beginning of the formation of the basic **ST Counter Direct Movement Pattern**. Both Corridors and their levels are active. Then, Corridor № 3 appears below Turn Level 2, and the price again turns up.

After breaking the Corridor № 3 upward, the position open down is closed. At the same time, a new deal opens upstairs. In this case, all three corridors do not violate Stop Levels. Accordingly, all three Corridors are operating simultaneously. At the bottom of the price, only Target Level 2 is waiting, and there is no alternative. And, if the market goes up, where will this pattern end? At Target Level 1 or Target Level 3?

In this situation, the bears could not completely repel the offensive of the bulls. Fixed above the level of Start Line 1, the bulls again went on the attack upward. With such a development of events, the probability of reaching

Target Level 1 remains high. Also, the completion of this model often occurs at this initial level. Figure 20 shows this pattern on a real price chart.

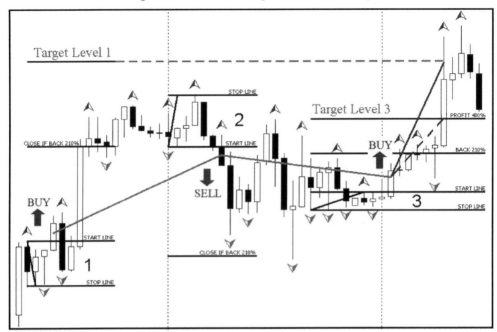

Figure 20: ST Direct Movement with Counter Movement Pattern

The higher the Start Line Level of Corridor № 1 is formed by Corridor № 3, the stronger the price movement upward with the onset of bulls. On the chart it is visible how this model, as with the ST Interrupt Direct Movement Pattern, ends at the level of the original Target.

Now consider ST Counter Movement with Direct Movement Pattern (Figure 21).

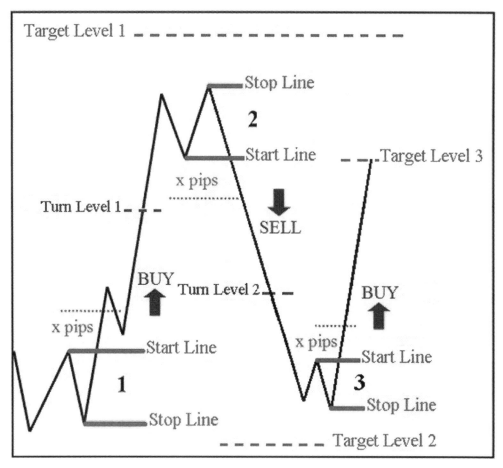

Figure 21: Scheme ST Counter Movement with Direct Movement Pattern

In this situation, the bulls were dropped below the level of the initial Start Line 1. Corridor № 3 was formed within the boundaries of Corridor № 1. The initial move up from Start Line 1 demonstrates its weakness. In this case, it is better to focus on the levels built from Corridor № 3. Moreover, it is more reliable to close the deal after the second purchase at Target Level 3. You can see how Corridors № 2 and № 3 formed the basic **ST Counter Direct Movement Pattern**.

The Target Level 1 value in this situation is also weakened due to the closing of some of the positions at breakeven level. Figure 22 shows the ST Counter Movement with Direct Movement Pattern that was shown in the *Forex Strategy* book when analyzing the EUR/USD pair.

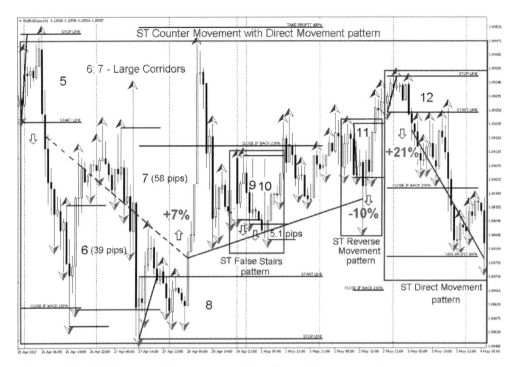

Figure 22: ST Counter Movement with Direct Movement Pattern

The downward movement began after the penetration of Corridor № 5. After a strong bullish counterattack at a level of 210%, the bears were driven back up and went on the offensive for the last time from the Corridor № 12. At that point, the level of the Start Line of Corridor № 12 is higher than the Start Line level of the initial Corridor № 5. This circumstance indicates the weakness of the bears and reduces the likelihood of reaching the original Target 5 price.

The day after the close of the position at 400% of the height of Corridor № 12 was followed by steady EUR growth, which confirmed the correctness of setting the Target at the level of 400% from the height of Corridor № 12.

Sometimes there are situations when Corridor № 3 is located in such a way that it is difficult to determine on which side the superior forces are located. In this case, you can use mixed tactics. Part of the position closes at Target Level 3, and the rest closes at Target Level 1.

Sometimes, when Corridor № 3 is formed, Target Level 3 exceeds the Target Level of Corridor № 1. In this situation, it is more reliable to close the position at Target Level 1. If the ratio of profit to loss is less than 2:1, the risk becomes too high to open a position. It is better to observe this rule for opening transactions.

Sometimes a higher Stop Line at Corridor № 1 forms more Counter Movements. To determine the Target Level in this situation, with the continuation of the initial movement, it is also better to take into account the correlation of the forces of bulls and bears.

The features of the models above should be considered when working with the ST Zero with Direct Movement Pattern, if the trader decides to use this model in his strategy. It should be noted that when working with this pattern it is also better not to open the opposite initial position within the boundaries of Corridor № 1 before the price reaches its Stop Line Level. The struggle between bulls and bears within the boundaries of the current Corridor is often fierce, with varying success and unpredictable results.

In volatile markets, such as the GBP/USD currency pair, there often appear sweeping models in which the oncoming traffic overcomes the Stop Line Level of the operating Corridor completing their action. The ST Two Counter Movements Pattern is shown in Figure 23.

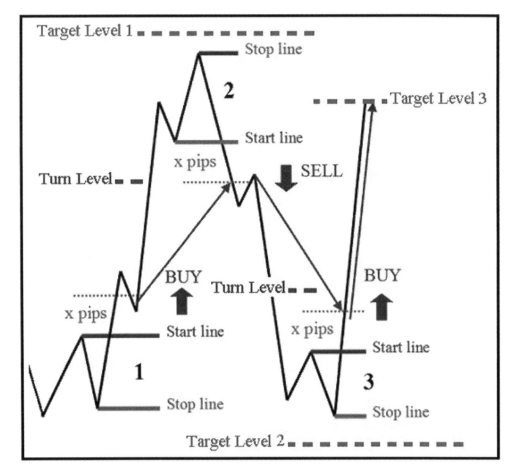

Figure 23: ST Two Counter Movements Pattern

Corridor № 1 ceases to operate at the moment the price crosses the level of Stop Line 1. All rights go to Corridor № 2. When Corridor № 3 appears, its levels also become effective. The model is completed after reaching the Target Level 3 price. Figure 24 displays the ST Three Counter Movements Pattern on a real chart.

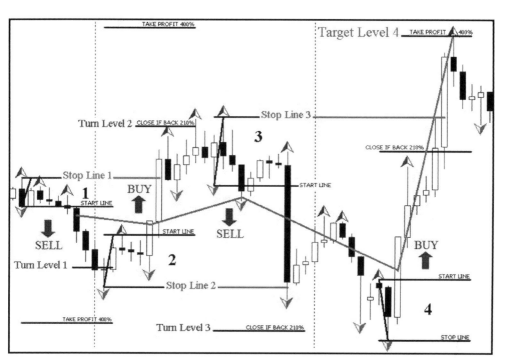

Figure 24: ST Three Counter Movements Pattern

Every time the price crosses the Stop Line of the previous Corridor, the last one loses its value and the Target Level is measured from the height of the last working Corridor. The model ends when the **ST Direct Movement Pattern** reaches its Target at 400% of the height of Corridor № 4.

To conclude the description of the features of the formation of ST Patterns, Figure 25 shows the ST Zero Pattern.

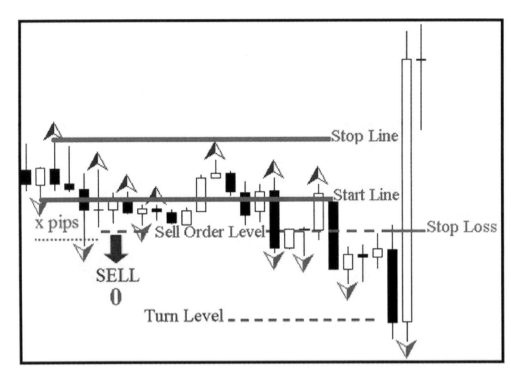

Figure 25: ST Zero Pattern

If you exclude the release of important economic news from the game, then moving the Stop Loss Order to a level without loss may be premature. Also, this technique can be ineffective in highly volatile markets, for example, GBP/USD.

Analysis of the EUR/USD Currency Pair

Next, one of the variants of ST Patterns Strategy work on the EUR/USD chart for the period from July 1 to August 31, 2017 will be shown. To begin, we set the parameters of the trading system.

The Level of Breakdown is equal to 7.6 pips. After the breakthrough of the Fractal Level, the opening of transactions will occur in deferred Limit Orders. To buy, set the Buy Limit Order at the Start Line Level plus 7 pips, and when selling, set the Sell Limit Order at the Start Line Level minus 6 pips.

It is more logical not to put the Take Profit Order exactly on the round levels as most players want. It is better to be among the first buyers than to defend a long queue and see how the goods ended right before you. When buying, we will place the Take Profit Order at 400% minus 2 pips, and when selling, we will set it at 400% plus 3 pips, given an assumed spread equal to 1 pip.

As before, the possible loss in one transaction will be established as equal to 10% of the amount of the trade deposit at the time of opening the transaction. When buying, the Stop Loss Order is set to the level of Stop Line + 1pips, and when selling, it is set exactly to the Stop Line Level. If we exclude periods of high volatility from the game, the Stop Order can be placed even closer to the price of entering the market when important economic indicators appear.

We will open a counter transaction after reaching the Turn Level price of 210% and until the execution of the Take Profit Order, while closing the previous position. Thus, for the whole analysis period only one position will be opened, or there will be no open positions at all.

The working hours for EUR/USD fall on the European and American trading sessions and last from 06 to 19 GMT. At night, this pair has low liquidity. The movements that occur between 20 and 05 GMT, as a rule, do not reflect the mood of market participants; therefore, it is not advisable to open a deal at this time. It is worth noting that the markets are filled with liquidity during trading session business hours, and this may vary from individual instruments. In non-working hours, there are rarely profitable ST Patterns, and at this time it is better to rest along with the market.

As before, we miss Corridors with a height of more than half of the five-day ADR. In this case, this indicator includes short Sundays. Some brokers may not show these days separately. In this case, to determine the large corridors, you can take a slightly smaller value than ADR (5) / 2.

Also, we do not work with Corridors with a height of less than 12 pips, and, accordingly, the ratio of profit to loss is less than 2 to 1. Apparently, the exchange market is not an exception to the rule of the golden mean. By following the "median way," you can get better results than by using all of the situations in a row. The ADR indicator can be found here: http://stpatterns.com/indicators-parameters/.

Economic news, coming out on schedule, can have a significant impact on the results of short-term trading. The state of affairs of the American economy has the strongest effect on the direction of the movement of exchange instruments. The amount of the interest rate is the main indicator of this. At the same time, the very decision to change rates is usually not a surprise. The subsequent press conference and forecasts regarding further actions by the regulator play a significant role. Sometimes the market pauses for a day or two before waiting for important decisions about future FRS policy.

The most important indicators influencing the decision to raise or lower the key rate are the employment indicators in the US; the main one is the unemployment rate. However, on the day of its publication, there are usually many other important indicators. As a rule, the release of this news usually occurs on a Friday. The next business day after the publication of this indicator, market participants study the analyses of economists and the comments of monetary authorities regarding the prospects for interest rate changes in the US and additional monetary policy changes.

To exclude this period of uncertainty from work, it is better to be out of the market on the day that the unemployment rate is published and on the next business day following its release. To a lesser extent, other economic indicators can also influence the market. Sometimes, when their value differs significantly from the forecast, sudden movements of quotations are possible. The market response to data that does not differ significantly from the forecast is different than the market response to data that either coincides with the forecast or differs significantly from it. In the case of the simultaneous release of several indicators, their coherence with each other matters.

To demonstrate the work of the purely technical part of the ST Patterns Strategy, we will avoid a deeper analysis of daily economic news and just exclude the publication day of the US unemployment rate and the next business day following its release. For the rest of the working time within the two-month period, we will open transactions, as would be done by a trading robot.

For a better understanding of the rules for building ST Patterns, it is advisable to independently check all the results below using your broker's charts. By studying the graphs one can also find some that are not relevant for calculating Fractal Corridors and these are not in the description. The graphics below are also available on Google Drive at: https://drive.google.com/drive/folders/0B3brjTjlH1PIdVBWVDVQZkxkems?usp=sharing

To simplify the analysis and demonstrate various variants of the ST Patterns Strategy, we will not transfer the Stop Loss Order to the level without loss upon reaching the price at the Turn Level.

Figure 26 shows the EUR/USD pair chart for the period from June 30 to July 6.

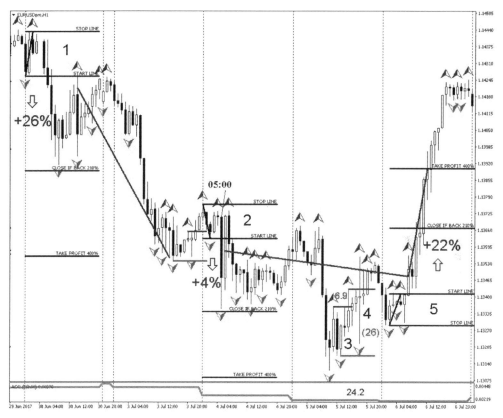

Figure 26: The EUR/USD pair chart for the period from June 30 to July 6

Everything is simple here. The ST Direct Movement Pattern brings +26%. It is followed by a profitable ST Counter Direct Movement Pattern. Following the ST False Movement Pattern with Corridor № 3 at the base, the Large

41

Corridor № 4 appears (the calculation of the ADR(5/2) indicator includes a short Sunday day, but some brokers do not show this short day).

The next day, July 7, the current unemployment rate in the United States and many other indicators are published. Accordingly, we should not open transactions until Tuesday. At the same time, we take into account the ST Patterns that appear during the long weekend.

The history of the formation of Corridor № 6 in the period from July 7-10 is shown in Figure 27.

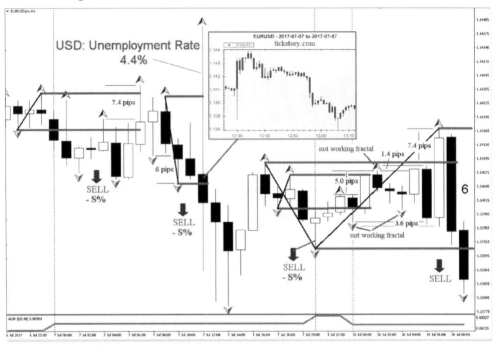

Figure 27: Formation of Corridor № 6

The unemployment rate in the US came out below the forecast. At the time of the release of the indicator and the next business day, the dynamics of the market were multidirectional. By the end of the day on Monday, the downward trend was determined. Work in this period could bring three losing trades in a row. Figure 28 shows the period from July 7-13.

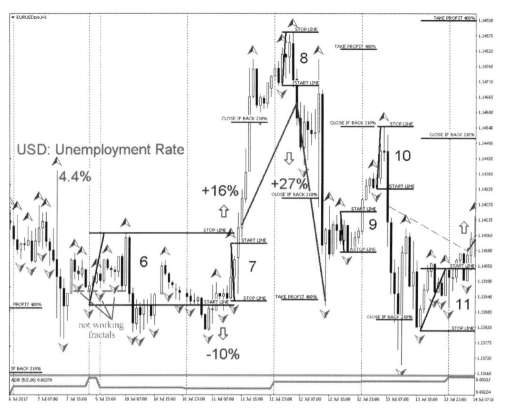

Figure 28: The EUR/USD pair chart for the period from July 7-13

We enter the market on July 11 at 06:00 GMT. However, the sale from the Start Line Level of Corridor № 6 was prematurely yielding a loss of 10%. Published at 14:00 GMT, the indicator Jolts Job Openings (May) was less than the forecast, which weakened the position of the US currency. Often the publication of this parameter leads to the beginning of directed movement after a given period of uncertainty. Therefore, rather than beginning trading at the start of the day, you should begin trading after the release of this indicator. Opening a position earlier can lead to a loss that can be avoided.

The ST Complex Reverse Movement Pattern with Corridor № 7 at the bottom develops, but the price does not reach Target Level 7. The ST Direct Movement Pattern starts down from the Corridor № 8 boundary and brings +27% at the Target Level 8 level. At this point, the profitable ST Counter Direct Movement Pattern is completed.

Corridor № 9 was punctured during non-working hours. At the beginning of the working day on July 13, the price reached the level of 210% of its height. The reverse movement from Corridor № 10 was swift. Minimal price rollback after the breakdown of the Fractal Level did not allow us to open the position down. Crossing the Stop Line Level of Corridor № 9 ceased its existence. Self-movement down is interrupted by a breakthrough to the top of Corridor № 11. In the future, Corridor № 10 together with Corridor № 11 will form another ST Counter Direct Movement Pattern.

Figure 29 shows the period from July 14-20.

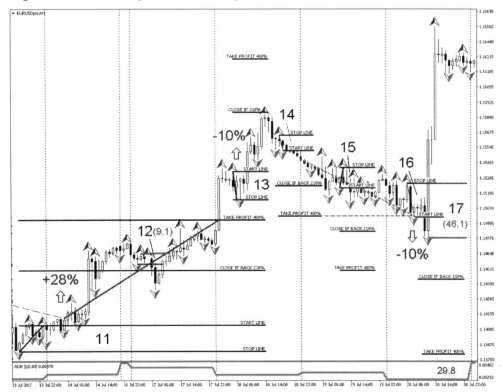

Figure 29: The EUR/USD pair chart for the period from July 14-20

The model was completed when the price reached the July 18 Target at Corridor № 11, yielding 28%. Corridor № 12 was missed because its height was 9.1 pips.

The move up from Corridor № 13 turned down to 210% without reaching 2 pips. Therefore, the position down from the Start Line of the Corridor № 14 does not open. Corridor № 13 loses its value after receiving a loss. The ST Complex Reverse Movement Pattern starts from the last Fractal Level of Corridor № 15, which was punched before the Stop Loss Order. However, the Target Level of 400% of the height of Corridor № 14 is very close to Corridor № 15. In this case, the value of the possible profit is approximately equal to the possible loss. Therefore, it is better to skip the deal in the lower direction.

After reaching a price level of 400% of the height of Corridor № 14, a new position was opened down from Corridor № 16. Released at 12:30 GMT, the Philadelphia Fed Manufacturing Index (July) was significantly below the forecast and quickly weakened the dollar, bringing a loss of 10% of the deposit. Corridor № 17 is too large.

Figure 30 shows the period from July 21-25.

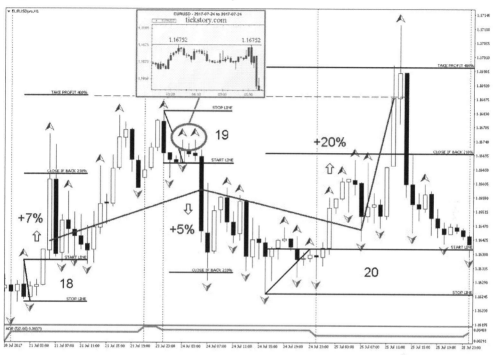

Figure 30: The EUR/USD pair chart for the period from July 21-25

Within three working days, a profitable ST Direct Movement with Counter Movement Pattern is formed. The Target is located at the level of 400% of the height of Corridor № 18. The charts for different brokers may differ. For someone in the red-highlighted zone, the left fractal will be 0.1 to 0.2 pips lower or higher than the right one. Differences in brokerage quotations can be taken into account by laying a predetermined error in the trading system, which can be individual in each specific case.

Figure 31 shows the period from July 26-31.

Figure 31: The EUR/USD pair chart for the period from July 26-31

Reaching the price of the Stop Loss Level at Corridor № 21 brings the ST Complex Reverse Pattern. Uncertainty in the market in anticipation of the release of important data brings a loss of 10%. At 18:00 GMT, the Fed Interest Rate Decision and FOMC Statement were published. A fast ST Direct Movement Pattern with Corridor № 22 at the base gives +26%.

At 06:00 GMT the next business day, the price is in the middle of the Corridor № 23. The loss could be 6% if you calculate the open position value from the Buy Order Level of this Corridor.

Corridor № 25 exposes its Target Level after the oncoming traffic reaches the Stop Loss Order Level of Corridor № 24 and erases its value. Closing the position brings +22%.

The EUR/USD pair chart for the period from July 31 through August 2 is shown in Figure 32.

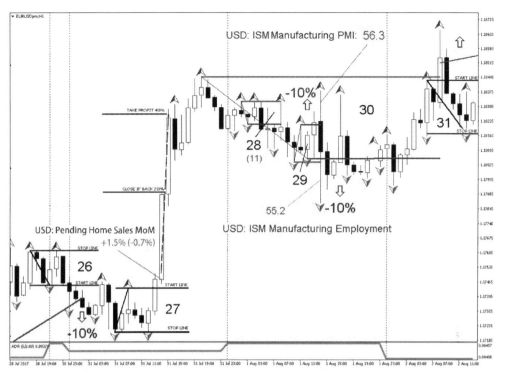

Figure 32: The EUR/USD pair chart for the period from July 31-August 2

Corridor № 26 did not last long. At 14:00 GMT Pending Home Sales (MoM) (Jun) data were published which were significantly higher than the previous value. Turning up, the price has reached the Target Level of 400% from the height Corridor № 27.

On August 1 at 14:00 GMT, four US economic indexes are published. The most important of these are the ISM Manufacturing Purchasing Managers Index (PMI) and the ISM Manufacturing Employment (July). The first indicator was below expectations, and the second is the higher one. As a result, the market could not choose a direction and drew an ST Double Reverse Movement Pattern. It was possible to avoid a double loss by not opening transactions during the publication of multidirectional indicators of significant economic data.

Figure 33 shows the period from August 2-4.

47

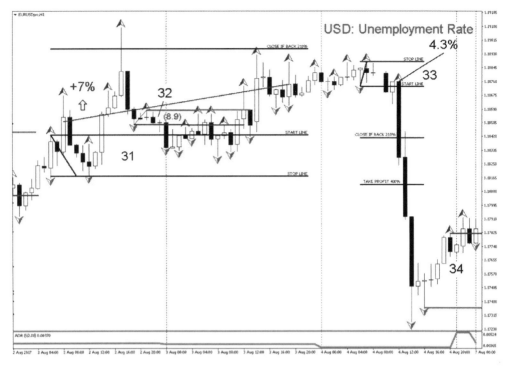

Figure 33: The EUR/USD pair chart for the period from August 2-4

Opened on August 2, the position to the top should be closed on August 3 at the end of the working day on the bottom of the 19-hour candle. Corridor № 32 is 8.9 pips. We do not open positions for the next four days due to the publication of the unemployment rate and other important data in the US.

At 12:30 GMT on August 24, ten economic indicators in the US are published. The most important of them, the unemployment rate, coincided with the forecast of 4.3%. The remaining indicators were equal to the forecast or better. All published data indicated a strengthening of the dollar. Theoretically, in such a situation, there was enough time to analyze the published indicators and open the position down.

However, for the accuracy of calculating the operation of the system, we will not violate the initial terms of trade. You can look at this possibility yourself on the five-minute EUR/USD charts.

Figure 34 shows the period from August 7-9.

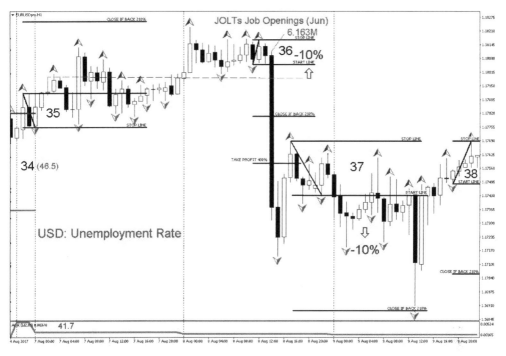

Figure 34: The EUR/USD pair chart for the period from August 7-9

The trading day starts at 06 GMT on August 8. Set the Buy Limit Order at the Start Line Level of Corridor № 35 plus 7 pips. However, at 14:00 the indicator Jolts Job Openings (June) is published, and it is better than the forecast.

In such a situation, the dollar receives an unambiguous signal to strengthen, and opening up the position is very dangerous. Do not rush under a racing truck, even if you are right and have been waiting for a long time at a pedestrian crossing. After purchase, the technical trading system, without taking into account the yield of important economic indicators, gives -10%. The next position, open from the level of Corridor № 37, brings another loss of -10%.

This is the fourth loss since the beginning of the month. In such periods, optimism about the successful operation of the system may begin to decrease.

Figure 35 shows the period from August 7-9.

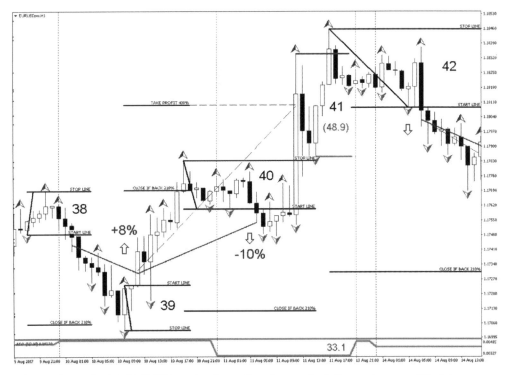

Figure 35: The EUR/USD pair chart for the period from August 10-14

The penetration of Corridor № 38 occurred during non-working hours, and it was not possible to open the position down. Having overcome the Turn Level of 210%, the price turned up and reached the level of the Stop Loss Order at Corridor № 38. At that moment, Corridor № 38 lost its value. Now, the main Target has moved to the level of 400% of the height of Corridor № 39.

On August 11, after crossing the level of 210% of the height of Corridor № 39, a downward movement occurs. Close the deal with the result +8%. Opening the position down brings a loss of 10%. The Core CPI (MoM) (July) released in the US at 12:30 GMT weakened the USD position above the Target level of 400% from the height of Corridor № 39. Corridor №s 38, 39, and 40 formed another ST Counter Interrupted Direct Movement Pattern.

It took almost half a month, but the result did not improve. Belief in the ability of a trading strategy to generate revenue can end prematurely at this stage. In such periods, many have thoughts about revising the parameters of the trading strategy or completely abandoning it. This is one of many psychological difficulties that a trader can experience.

Figure 36 shows the EUR/USD pair chart from August 14-18.

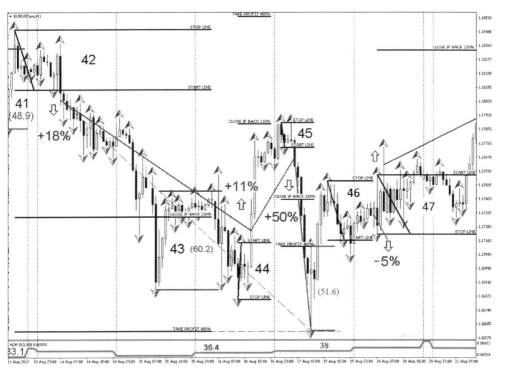

Figure 36: The EUR/USD pair chart for the period from August 14-18

Within four days, the ST Direct Movement with Counter Movement Pattern was formed. Corridor № 45 formed below the Start Line at Corridor № 42. This means the bears are strong and continue their offensive to the level of 400% of the height of Corridor № 42. Mass profit-taking by players stops the price drop at the Target level plus 1.2 pips, which allows us to close the position with an excellent result: +50% of the deposit. This is a good bonus for those who remained faithful to the trading system, despite a short period of losses.

The beginning of the workday on August 18 is shown in Figure 37.

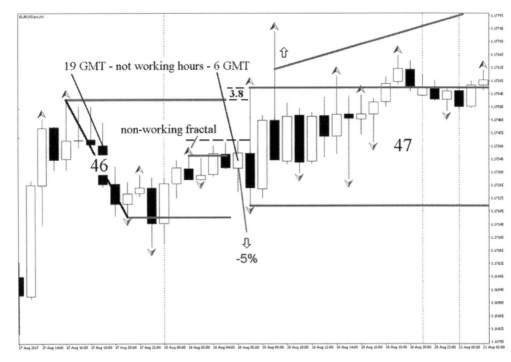

Figure 37: Schedule EUR/USD, 30M

The graph shows how Corridor № 47 was formed. The loss could be 5% if you calculate the open position value from the Sell Order Level at Corridor № 46.

Figure 38 shows the period from August 18-25.

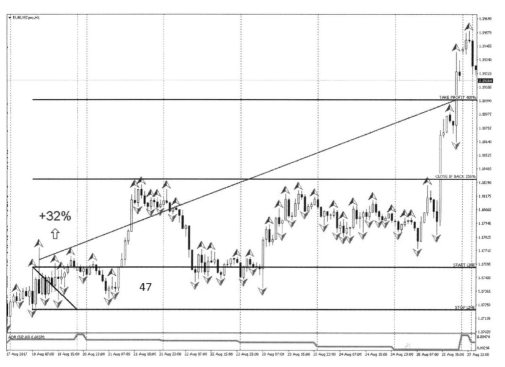

Figure 38: The EUR/USD pair chart for the period from August 18-25

A long ST Direct Movement Pattern is formed in anticipation of the annual symposium of the Fed in Jackson Hole. On August 25, market participants, who were expecting Janet Yellen's statements to continue the process of raising rates, were disappointed, and the price reached the Target with a result of +32%. Figure 39 shows the period from August 28-31.

Figure 39: The EUR/USD pair chart for the period from August 28-31

Two profitable ST Direct Movement Patterns complete the demonstration of the model's work. At 22:00 GMT on August 28, a breakthrough of the Fractal Level did not take place. The ST False Movement Pattern shown in the upper right corner of the chart overcame the lower fractal by 0.4 pip and made it invalid when the price moved down.

To calculate the final result, we add all the percentages shown in the graphs for the full two months to the initial deposit, for example, 1000 conventional units. 1000 + 26% + 4% + 22% - 10% + 16% + 27% + 28% -10% - 10% + 7% + 5% + 20% - 10% + 26% - 6% + 2% + 22% - 10% - 10% - 10% + 7% - 10% - 10% + 8% - 10% + 18% + 11% + 50% - 5% + 32% + 26% + 30% = 9740 conventional units or approximately + 874% to the amount of the initial deposit.

54

For comparison, you can calculate the results for each month separately: July + 238%, August + 190%. These data show that the progression built in two months yields almost twice as much than the withdrawal tactics from the monthly profit account. However, income is often associated with risk. In the event of a freelance situation on the market, for example, a gap, the loss will be proportional to the value of the open position. Breaks in prices in liquid markets, though rare, do sometimes occur.

These dangerous moments, as a rule, result from the release of important, unexpected news. The market is particularly vulnerable when it opens after the weekend. Each trader chooses his own tactics of action, including the approach to managing capital. Often, the truth is in the middle, but each has his own.

Such results were obtained during the development of market movements without taking into account the impact of a great deal of important economic news on trade. A trading robot could obtain this profit at this point in time, if it was working without errors. If, on the other hand, you exclude unprofitable trades done without considering the analysis of important economic news, the result could be much better.

As noted above, the main impact on the exchange movements of currency pairs directly related to the dollar comes from publications of data about the labor market in the United States. They, in turn, are the most important indicators for the decision to change interest rates. Sometimes, following comments from financial regulators, other economic indicators—for example, inflation—also receive a greater weight. The market begins to fever when important indicators differ significantly from the forecast, especially when they differ for the worse.

Periodically, the focus of market participants shifts to business in the Chinese economy or European countries. The market associated with European trading instruments may fall into a state of uncertainty, for example, from the possibility of defaults in Greece or Spain. Information on the increase in the pumping money into markets can give a start to the rally, which has recently been observed in the stock markets. Since 2009, there has been virtually no month of global markets without QE. When the Fed called an end to it, the Bank of Japan or the ECB started it.

For the commodity futures market, the important data are the indicators of warehouse stocks and other industry parameters. Many trading instruments are linked to each other through major currencies. However, they may be affected to varying degrees by economic and political factors. For example, the GBP/USD pair may be abandoned by the players, while the EUR/USD pair will actively develop profitable graphic models.

If a trader does not have the desire or ability to monitor the impact that each indicator has on the market, he can simply exclude the important data from the trading days. In this case, there will be at least two weeks every month when the usual ST Patterns will appear on the charts.

The effect that periods of uncertainty caused by serious political events have on trading results was shown in the example of GBP/USD movements in the *Forex Strategy* book.

The examples of the work of the ST Patterns Strategy in three books prove its working capacity and high efficiency. Of the dozens of known and not very popular trading strategies, I have not seen a single one capable of showing at least some of the results demonstrated by this system.

Mind and Subconscious

Any, even the best, trading system cannot work independently. Success on the stock exchange, first of all, depends on the trader's ability to apply his system in practice. The basic emotions that arise when working with the ST Patterns Strategy were written about in the *Trading Code is Open* book. There are also general psychological problems that are independent of a particular strategy.

The market is always right

About ten years ago, I witnessed a curious but instructive case. My friend asked me to help him to understand what had happened in his recently opened financial company. The fact is that not long after the commencement of work the trading account to which a large amount of money was initially transferred was suddenly empty.

Account management was led by two traders who were certified to work in the financial markets and who purported to be professionals in their business. However, they could not give clear explanations for the misunderstanding that had occurred. After studying the history of the transactions, I realized what had happened. Not long after they bought shares with a small leverage, the market, contrary to expectations, began to move in the direction of the protective stop order.

Next, for about a month, the protective suspension was simply moved away from the market, which persistently tried to get it, and then it was completely taken away. They tried to save the loss position with the help of more risky financial instruments of futures and options. As a result, this entire built pyramid was closed forcibly by the Margin call rules broker. The initially planned, long-term conservative work strategy turned into a very risky occupation within a month. Unwillingness to take a loss on time can be expensive.

Prediction of the future

For successful stock trading, you do not need to be a predictor of the direction of the price movement. Do not also persist in your belief, if the market is not moving in the right direction. The market is always right. It is like a spontaneous phenomenon that can sweep up everything in its path. The ST Patterns Strategy follows market movements according to their actual occurrence and is not predictive, unlike most other methods of technical analysis.

If you do not have the capacity for predictions, like Vanga, then you can hardly rely on visionary clairvoyance. In this case, voices in your head suggesting what you need to do, most likely, will belong to greed and fear, which are bad advisers on the market. It is necessary to execute the trading system automatically, not letting your emotions impose themselves on your opinion. This is one of the main difficulties that prevents traders from observing and executing a planned strategy.

The Survival Instinct

The survival instinct is a basic component of the human, so emotional impulses often emerge from it. They are difficult to control with the help of the mind. Not many people are able to remain calm in the face of danger. The influx of adrenaline into the blood after the opening of a major transaction can completely overshadow the mind. Examples of the work of the ST Patterns Strategy were shown using a 10% loss. However, a 2-3% loss will significantly reduce the psychological stress and make trade more comfortable.

Belief in the Trading System

Another primary component of success is one's belief in the trading system. In this case, the market is arranged so that the losses alternate with the gains. Every loss undermines faith and lays an Engram, and if the mind cannot understand how the exchange is arranged, the subconscious perceives each loss as a danger. After even small accidents, many drivers begin to drive more carefully, but some completely refuse to drive again. Having lost faith in the trading system, you can miss a profitable deal.

Superfluous Transactions

At the same time, the saying "too much water drowned the miller" reflects the situation in which transactions are opened too often. If you use all the opportunities for opening positions, the results can be worse than if you enter the market less often but only during quiet periods.

A separate book about the influence that emotions have on the irrational actions of traders could be written, but this has already been done by Dr. Elder and many others. Exchange trade is a work in which the mind, will, exact calculation, speed of reaction, patience, willpower, and other qualities that are not often encountered in one person are required. I think that traders with experience know this well. Beginning players need to consider this circumstance when opening a real account with a broker in the hopes of a high profit.

Before you decide to apply the ST Patterns Strategy in practice, it is desirable to get positive results for at least two months working on a demo account!

Answer to the Question

Sometimes I'm asked the following: Why do you share a profitable strategy? At first, I also thought that the system might not continue to work properly after I had published it. But then it became clear that my modest book would not change the situation. It couldn't compete with marketing companies' selling strategies, analyses, and trading signals. Advertisements on well-known financial platforms cost tens and hundreds of thousands of dollars a month.

Brokers and financial companies spend a lot of money and efforts to attract customers, offering advice and help from titled specialists. Many forums for traders are crowded with sellers of services, goods, and paid coaches. On some of them, my profile was immediately blocked after I placed several charts demonstrating how the ST Patterns Strategy works. In the field of investment, there are also a lot of swindlers who do not hesitate in their promises, offering easy profits in the hope of capturing their clients' money.

Thus, many traders continue to donate their deposits in the name of widely advertised trading methods, even if these methods do not work. There are millions of traders and thousands of trading systems in the world. It takes years to study at least a dozen well-known strategies and their application in practice. Most players, having lost their deposits several times over, will forever leave the stock exchange.

But even if the ST Patterns Strategy starts to be applied by several thousand traders, that will only make it more effective. Within four months of the publication of the first book, approximately 200 people became acquainted with this strategy. Of these, only 10-20% can profitably use it. To some it will seem too complicated, and others will be disturbed by emotions and lack of discipline.

Thus, the excess of traders in the market using this one strategy will not happen very quickly, if such is ever possible. And if the market changes, you can always pick the best variable parameters for the trading strategy, change the rules for working with models, or switch to another trading tool. Now, for the first time, I will check the graph of the popular crypt currency Bitcoin using ST Patterns. The BTC/USD M5 chart is shown in Figures 40 and 41.

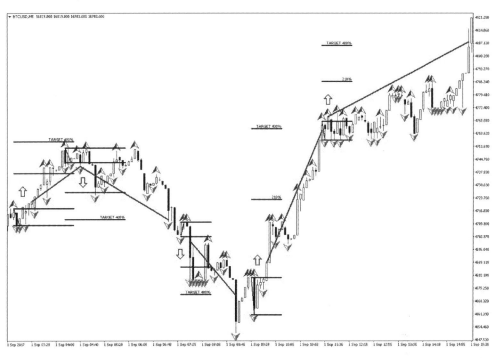

Figure 40: Chart BTC/USD, M5, September 1, 2017

Figure 41: Chart BTC/USD, M5, September 1, 2017

A quick analysis of this graph allows you to see a familiar picture. This crypto currency is rapidly changing. Therefore it's probably better to use a percentage of the corridor's height rather than a fixed value for a breakthrough. Of course, in order to start real trading, you need to spend more time studying the features of each instrument and selecting the optimal parameters. However, the basic meaning of speculative work, which is laid out in the ST Patterns Strategy, should remain the same. The wavy structure of market charts will always be a reflection of the presence of traders in the market who will open deals at critical moments and then fix profits at the Target level.

Conclusion

In conclusion, I would like to sincerely thank the people who helped me in my work on all three books. Of course, first of all, my wife and daughter, for moral support and all-round help. Sarah Zurhellen for responsible work on editing the text. My school friend Dmitriy Kisil, for the words of support.

Thanks to all the traders who shared their feedback and questions with me. I would like to express special gratitude to Dr. Alexander Elder, George Socina, Jim Brown, Steve Fleming, Bruno Mothes, Matteo Cirulli, David Ankrapp, Ahmed M., Ossama Omar, Bart Van Vriesland, Eddie Chee, Ranjit Bajaj, Venkat Yerram, Keaka O'Ryan, Charles A. Floyd, II and others. I would like to express special thanks to Hiroshi Sekiguchi, who carefully studied all three of my books. His clever and detailed questions helped me to make more correct and clear definitions in the description of the strategy.

Without your advice and participation, I probably would not have written and published the second and third books. The feedback and opinions gave me enthusiasm for the writing and pointed out important topics for coverage.

Dear Collegian traders and readers! I have shared with you most of my knowledge gained over my years of work in the market. Unfortunately, there is no simple way that can guarantee a 100% profit and safety from all losses. I hope that my books are able to help traders cut their path in a difficult direction toward financial freedom. I wish you many profitable graphic models. Good luck!

I am grateful for any feedback left at the place of purchase of this book. ST Patterns are enough for everyone!

Contact

Send your questions, wishes, and suggestions through the feedback form on the website: http://stpatterns.com.

Printed in Great Britain
by Amazon